THE LAST CHAPTER

Understanding Where We Go When We Die

Paul C Moore

The Last Chapter

AUTHORED BY:
Paul C Moore

EDITED BY:
Paul and Kip Moore

PRINTED BY AUTHOR MEDIA DESIGN
authormediadesign.com

DEDICATION

This book is dedicated to my Father in Heaven for showing me that he loves me and that I can trust him.

CONTENTS

Introduction

There is a lot of controversy surrounding death, hell, and the afterlife. Many people who attend religious institutions have a belief in a place of eternal torment and punishment of fire and flame where people go to writhe in agony being poked by the devil and his pitchfork. They teach that if you don't say the Sinner's Prayer that you will wind up in hell for eternity.

Does saying a repeat-after-me prayer really ensure that a person goes to heaven to be with God and the angels? What I understand from some of the people I went to church with is that not only will you not go to heaven if you don't say the sinner's prayer, but if you smoke a cigarette, or have a drink of alcohol, or listen to rock and roll music, your place will be with the devil and his angels. You will burn forever in this eternal abode for drinking, smoking, and listening to certain types of music. And the only exception is if you listen to worship music?

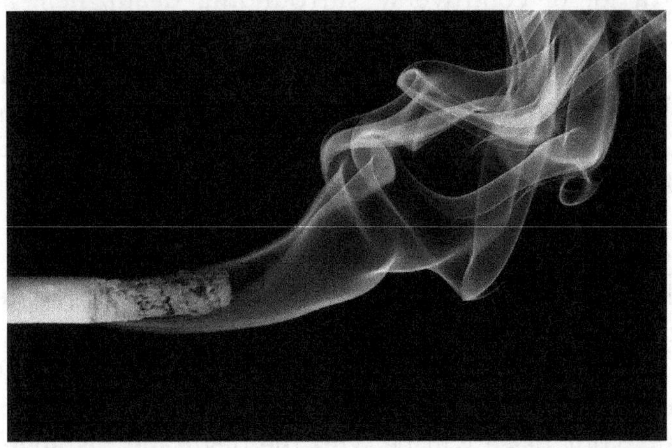

What I learned is that there are much more weighty matters to being in a relationship with God than having a drink, cigarette, or listening to rock and roll music. Those things on their own are not a problem for God, but if you indulge in smoking or drinking, there may be a chance that you get to the other side sooner than you anticipated.

If Heaven is our final destination of peace, harmony, abundance, happiness, and all those other wonderful things, why does nobody want to go there? Why are we so afraid of dying? I mean if it such a great place why does the notion of death scare us so much? I believe in the reality of heaven, but I think for many the topic is unknown to most people and therefore people fear what they do not know. In other words, they have a great fear of the unknown.

There is no fear in death.

In this teaching, you will learn where we go after we die and why we go there. We will learn the truth about the afterlife as I have ascertained from God during my quiet times with him. You will learn how to have a happy life here on earth and on the other side of life too.

There is one scripture at the back of the Bible, the last chapter, that we are going to use as our text for this teaching. It's found embedded in the middle of the last chapter. What God has shown me is that many Christians, Muslims, and Jews will not like the reality of this scripture, because it will starkly show them the error of their ways if they wanted a relationship with God but exchanged it for religion.

Our Greatest Error

That will be the greatest error of most people who call themselves believers. They will come to the realization that their life in religion, going to a building, singing a few songs, passing around the hat, listening to a long boring message, singing a few more songs, was empty. Where does the Bible say that one must attend a corporate service to meet with God? Where does it say that?

Listen to me. A church, mosque, or synagogue service will never prepare anyone for a place inside the New Jerusalem. To get oneself inside the Holy City will take a lot of work, discipline, and diligence. Something sorely lacking in today's religious world. You can't expect God to open wide the floodgates of heaven to you if you never took the time to get to know him. There will be a lot of regrets when we stand before God because of this. How can singing songs, giving large amounts of money to a leader, listening to a hit or miss sermon, ever secure us a place of good standing in the here ever after?

Jesus, in his day, tried to show people what the Father was like, but many abandoned him too. So, if you don't like what you are going to learn in this teaching, you can't say that you weren't warned. God would like to see you in the next life happy and enjoying the paradise he has for you, but many will not enter in because of pride, arrogance, and a bad, know-it-all attitude. ****Newsflash!**** we know nothing! None of us. Zero. Zip. Nada. So, if you want to know what you must do in order to find yourself in a happy place on the other side of life, you are going to have to lose your attitude and become a diligent God-seeker. Not a goosebump seeker.

Let's get started.

Why I Wrote This Book

I wrote this book after some very startling revelations from God the Father. I never imagined him to be the person he has shown himself to be. I always thought he was out to hurt me and punish me for my sins. Little did I know it was not the Father who was out to punish me, as Jesus talked about, I was reaping what I sowed, or what goes around comes around, or what others call Karma.

Back in the day I was the proudest, arrogant, dumbest person who walked the earth. Then in 2011 I discovered a friend I never knew, and that was after twenty-seven years of calling myself a 'believer'. I call him 'Abba' which means 'Daddy'. In my thirty-seven years of knowing of God I never could trust him, because I thought if I made the ultimate mistake, he would send me off to hell to burn forever.

The Father wanted me to tell you that he is not angry with you. He is not out to get in the sense that he wants to do you harm, no, he wants to get you into his Kingdom, in this life and the next. He wants you to have an abundant life where you have everything you need to make you happy.

He wants you to walk away from reading this book knowing what it is you must do to find him. Yes, he has been seeking you for many years, and his desire is to have you for a good friend of his. He knows the reason why people are suffering so much on this planet have nothing to do with evil men or the devil, but everything to do with the reality that we have all forgotten the Father. He is reaching out to everyone because he wants his children back, ALL of them.

Why You Should Read This Book

We have been lied to – all of us. If you are tired of the hamster wheel of life and you want to get off the roller coaster you should read this book. It will help you immensely if you are willing to accept what the Father is trying to say to you in the words of these pages.

The journey of a thousand miles starts with a single step. God bless you.

THE LAST CHAPTER

Chapter One

We Have Been Doing It All Wrong!

God created life on earth for its inhabitants to enjoy the planet and have fun, yes, fun. But a lot of people aren't having fun these days. Many of us have been hurt and we are bitter, resentful, vengeful, jaded, and are experiencing a host of other negative emotions and behaviors. God understands that, and he wants to help us to enjoy our lives to the fullest. Albert Einstein said that insanity is defined as doing the same thing over and over again, expecting different results. It's time we got off the hamster wheel of holding bitterness and revenge towards those who have hurt us, either through perceptions or actual hurt. If what is being said here makes you want to close down and turn off the computer, may I suggest you go through my course entitled, 'Heal Our Broken Hearts', found at,

https://paulcmoore.ca/courses/heal-our-broken-hearts

Life was never meant to be bitter for us; it's just that life sent us some very serious blows in the formative years or even later years which caused us to shut down. Instead of being bitter, let's work together on being better. If you need help in this area we can talk. Message me with your contact info from my about page. I charge $25.00 an hour to mentor you.

So, our planet is filled with hurt and broken people and no one seems to know what to do with them. I was one of those people, no one that I reached out to for help gave the initiative to help me. There were a lot of Christian men who thought they knew what I needed to do but in hindsight, they were as broken as I was, or even more broken than me. The problem is that we have all these people roaming around in our Churches, Mosques, and Synagogues who have never been made disciples by anyone. We are all just treading water hoping someday to find a happy place to live with enough money to survive. God does not want us surviving, he wants us thriving. We were made to thrive on this planet and many of us are not even surviving. There are 800,000 suicides on the planet each year. It doesn't have to be this way. We were created for excellence and to have an abundance.

It Started with the Factories

As farmers and other business owners left the fields and shops for the security of working for the 'man', during the industrial revolution, the family unit started to disintegrate. Men worked long hours in exchange for security and lost their lives and families in the process. They loosened up on the weekend by consuming alcohol to relieve the stress of their weekday jobs. Whether it was under the ground working in a mine, or a car plant, or whatever else the 'man' wanted them to do.

As the marriage unit started collapsing, children fell into their father's footsteps, drinking, drugs, sexual immorality, stealing, and a whole host of other non-working behaviors. The prisons are full of delinquent children who never had a good father figure. There is a saying, *what parents do in moderation, children do to excess.* It's this excessive lifestyle that has brought many people down to an early grave, wandering to and fro, into and out of dead-end jobs and relationships. They are looking for something but have never found it.

I was one of those people, but I found it. I know what it is they are looking for and I found him. He is the only one who can put us back together. I'm not talking about Jesus here, I'm talking about his Father, God the Father. He is the only one who can put us back together. He is the only one who ever could. A Church service or Bible study can never mend a broken heart, regardless of how sincere the teacher is, only God the Father can mend our broken hearts, only the Father. I have been on this planet for close to six decades and I can attest that it was the Father, not Jesus, an angel, or anyone else who put me back together.

We all need a loving father.

So, humanity is still reeling from the industrial revolution. People are drifting off to eternity without ever knowing what could have been. We've all made a ton of mistakes in this life and our biggest mistake is that we never prepared for the afterlife. Mankind was never meant to die, but when sin was introduced mankind was never the same. God wants to restore his people's lives right back to the Garden of Eden. Having an abundance of all good things: money, health, happiness, joy unspeakable, sweet sleep, and dreams. It is not only possible to have this lifestyle on this side of life, but your Father in Heaven wants to make it possible for you.

If you want to know what the Father requires of you, the things that you must do, I *STRONGLY* suggest that you go through my course entitled, 'These Four Things', and learn the necessary habits to develop to make you a seasoned and wise believer. Here is the link: https://paulcmoore.ca/courses/these-four-things

Remember, if life isn't working for you now, what do you have to lose by changing a few things in your life to make yourself and others happier and more content? I've said this before, this isn't rocket science. In the next lesson, we are going to look at what is going to happen to people in the afterlife and what they can do about it.

Chapter Two

God wants to bless you abundantly, but it will take some time.

God is in the process of blessing people, but many choose bitterness over blessing and this will cause many to miss out when they stand before God at their judgment. There are only three places a person goes after they die,

1. The Lake of Fire
2. Outside the New Jerusalem
3. Inside the New Jerusalem

The Lake of Fire: This will be the place for the devil and his angels. They will burn for a long time in the Lake of Fire. When I was discouraged one day I said to the Father, "maybe you should just send me to the Lake of Fire." He said to me, "Paul, you don't want to go there." I could tell by his thoughts that the Lake of Fire is going to be a horrible place to go. I want to share something with you, He told me that under 1500 human beings from the beginning of time will be thrown into the Lake of Fire. For most people, they will not be sent to the Lake of Fire. Murders, rapists, pedophiles, thieves, and all others who committed heinous crimes will be spared the Lake of Fire. Why? It's because most people who committed those crimes were in complete and utter darkness and God will never punish anyone in that state who has committed these crimes by sending them to the Lake of Fire.

What about hell? Please watch the following video by George Carlin: Here is the link: https://youtu.be/8r-e2NDSTuE

God never created a place called hell.

This video may be offensive to some, but what Mr. Carlin presents in the first part of this video is a foundational truth about the nature of God. The bible says in 1John4,

Anyone who does not love does not know God, because God is love. 1John4 ESV

Mr. Carlin makes the case of how a loving God would take a human being who has made a ton of mistakes, like we all have made, and cast them into the Lake of Fire, for what? Not saying the 'sinner's prayer'? For not going to Church. Mosque? Synagogue? Temple? Really? Is that who God is? I don't think so, in fact, I know attendance in any type of religious institution does not warrant a place in the New Jerusalem. God is a loving parent who desires to have all of his children with him, but many will not come to him, so what will be their fate? There is an answer to that question, but many will not like the answer.

I'm trying to establish a fundamental principle that God's people, or those who say they follow God, have missed. If God is a loving father and loves us and will never leave us or forsake us, what pleasure will he take in seeing us suffer in this life and suffer for eternity, when we die? I'm sorry, but we have been lied to. If God takes no pleasure in seeing his children suffer, why would he want them to suffer for eternity, for making mistakes? Really?

"Well," says the haughty believer. "I followed Jesus and I accepted him into my heart when I was four years old and I followed him all of my life. I went to church, Bible studies, I headed the Men's Ministry, I brought four children into the world and taught them all about God and serving him. I have done so much for God and I know I will be there at his right hand in the Kingdom. Those Gays, drug addicts, drinkers and smokers, and all other vile people are going to HELL!!!"

Christmas: Real or imagined?

"Really? You foolish person, let me ask you a few questions:

Did you teach your children to lie?"

"Never!"

"Then why did you lie to them about Santa Claus? Why did you lie to them about the tooth fairy and the Easter bunny?

"But that was so the children could have fun there's nothing wrong with that!"

"You foolish person, you lied to your children! The first words out of your mouth concerning Christmas was that jolly old Saint Nick was going to come down the chimney, (which is impossible) and give your children a bunch of gifts."

"Yeah, but..."

"No buts, you lied and taught your children to lie. Who said you were to celebrate Christmas and Easter?"

"God commanded it. December 25 is the birth of Jesus and his resurrection is at Easter, everybody knows that are you stupid?!"

"Wrong again, you believed a lie and you taught this lie to others. Jesus was never born in December and Easter is a pagan holiday. Nowhere in my word does it say to celebrate Christmas and Easter. You foolish person, your life has been steeped in lies. You are a liar, and you do the work of your father, the devil, he is a liar and the father of lies."

"I'm not a liar! I love God!"

"If you loved me you would have kept my Commandments."

"Which ones?"

"All of them."

"Yeah, but which ones?"

"To keep the Sabbath and..."

"I kept the Sabbath; I went to church every Sunday!"

"Sunday is not the Sabbath..."

"So you're telling me we had to keep the Jewish stuff? I read the New book, not the Jew book!"

"And that my friend is why you may never see my face."

"Why? What have I done wrong...?"

Watch the truth about Christmas and Easter.

Here is the link: https://youtu.be/S8sKNOxyd8w

So, you can see that the haughty believer never learned the truth and became indignant with God and felt that God owed him because of the man's church attendance, tithing, celebrating Christmas and Easter, and many other pagan practices. If you feel you have arrived as a Christian, Muslim, or Jew, let me tell you something, you haven't. You know nothing. Like I said, none of us do. It's our spiritual pride and arrogance that keeps us out of the Kingdom of God. Our unwillingness to be taught and our false belief that we have arrived at a place where we know it all.

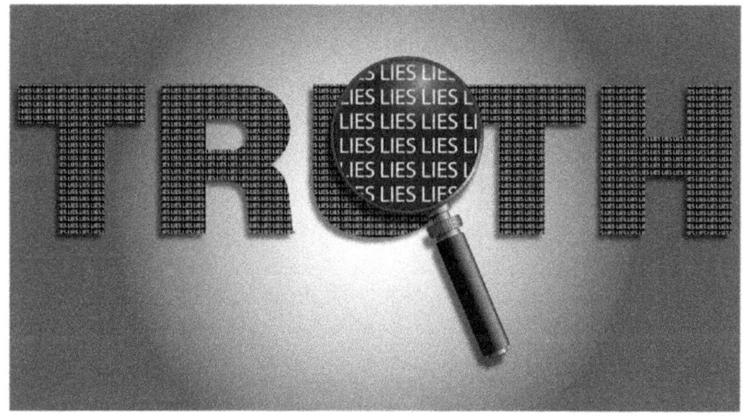

We never took the time to verify if our beliefs were based on truth or lies.

Humanity is steeped in lies, as the Bible says,

Darkness covers the earth and deep darkness the peoples. Isaiah 60:2

If we think that because we call ourselves Christians, Muslims, Jews, Hindus, or Buddhists that this scripture doesn't apply to us we are gravely mistaken. We are ALL steeped in darkness. If belonging to any of these religions brought peace and unity to the world, I would sign up right away, but as I said, the world is growing darker and darker and all of the 4 billion+ people on the planet who identify as some type of believer have done nothing to make a positive change on earth. The crimes we commit against each other in the name of God are so heinous it's a wonder God doesn't just pull the plug on the whole thing. We are so fragile, and this planet is only surviving by the grace of God. One worldwide drought could cause most of humanity to die. God doesn't want that for us, but at some point, we have to start doing things his way.

In conclusion, there is no hell, just the Lake of Fire, no eternal burning even if you wind up in the Lake of Fire. There an individual will burn and then eventually burn up until they become stubble. I don't know how long they will burn or if burning forever applies only to the devil and his angels. As I said God revealed to me that there will be less than 1500 human beings that will be sent to the Lake of Fire. In the next lesson, we will learn who goes to live inside the New Jerusalem. If you want to live in the New Jerusalem, you will have to invest in your future by doing things God's ways. Once on the other side, you will stand before God, and there is only one place you will want to find yourself, in the New Jerusalem.

Chapter Three

Here is the last chapter of the Bible:

1 And he shewed me a pure river of water of life, clear as crystal,
proceeding out of the throne of God and of the Lamb.

2 In the midst of the street of it, and on either side of the river, was
there the tree of life, which bare twelve manner of fruits, and
yielded her fruit every month: and the leaves of the tree were for
the healing of the nations.

3 And there shall be no more curse: but the throne of God and of the
Lamb shall be in it; and his servants shall serve him:

4 And they shall see his face; and his name shall be in their
foreheads.

5 And there shall be no night there; and they need no candle,
neither light of the sun; for the Lord God giveth them light: and
they shall reign for ever and ever.

6 And he said unto me, These sayings are faithful and true: and the
Lord God of the holy prophets sent his angel to shew unto his
servants the things which must shortly be done.

7 Behold, I come quickly: blessed is he that keepeth the sayings of
the prophecy of this book.

[8] And I John saw these things, and heard them. And when I had heard and seen, I fell down to worship before the feet of the angel which shewed me these things.

[9] Then saith he unto me, See thou do it not: for I am thy fellow servant, and of thy brethren the prophets, and of them which keep the sayings of this book: worship God.

[10] And he saith unto me, Seal not the sayings of the prophecy of this book: for the time is at hand.

[11] He that is unjust, let him be unjust still: and he which is filthy, let him be filthy still: and he that is righteous, let him be righteous still: and he that is holy, let him be holy still.

[12] And, behold, I come quickly; and my reward is with me, to give every man according as his work shall be.

[13] I am Alpha and Omega, the beginning and the end, the first and the last.

[14] Blessed are they that do his commandments, that they may have right to the tree of life, and may enter in through the gates into the city.

[15] For without are dogs, and sorcerers, and whoremongers, and murderers, and idolaters, and whosoever loveth and maketh a lie.

[16] I Jesus have sent mine angel to testify unto you these things in the churches. I am the root and the offspring of David, and the bright and morning star.

[17] And the Spirit and the bride say, Come. And let him that heareth say, Come. And let him that is athirst come. And whosoever will, let him take the water of life freely.

[18] For I testify unto every man that heareth the words of the prophecy of this book, If any man shall add unto these things, God shall add unto him the plagues that are written in this book:

[19] And if any man shall take away from the words of the book of this prophecy, God shall take away his part out of the book of life, and out of the holy city, and from the things which are written in this book.

[20] He which testifieth these things saith, Surely I come quickly. Amen. Even so, come, Lord Jesus.

[21] The grace of our Lord Jesus Christ be with you all. Amen.

The scripture I want to deal with concerning this chapter is verse 15,

For without are dogs, and sorcerers, and whoremongers, and murderers, and idolaters, and whosoever loveth and maketh a lie.

Before we deal with those on the outside, let's deal with those who are going to be on the inside of the New Jerusalem.

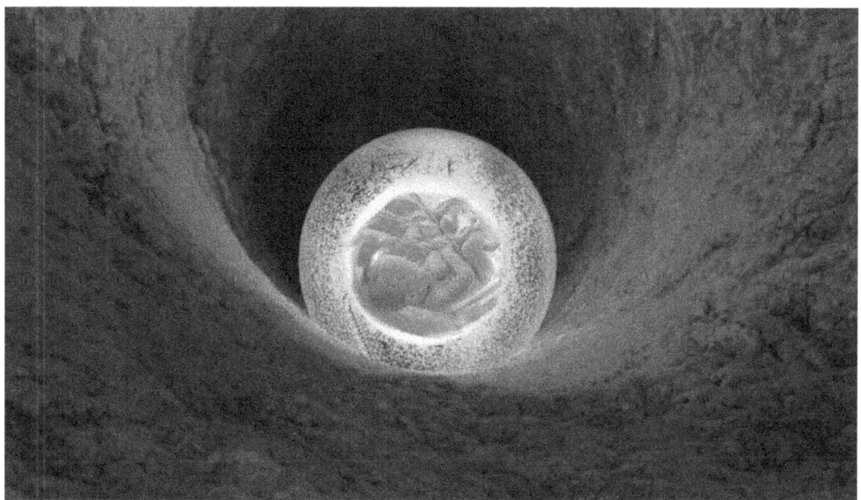

Life starts at conception.

According to what I heard from the Father is that most of the people who are in the New Jerusalem are children, about three trillion of them. They are the children who were murdered, aborted, tortured, and killed victims of satanic ritual abuse and other pagan sacrifices, and countless other ways that children have been annihilated. Every time a sperm united with an egg on earth if only for a moment, that person became a living being. I don't know how the embryo was formed after that, but according to God all of those children from abortion and other murders will be in the New Jerusalem.

What alarmed me the most about this discussion I had with God is that he told me only 3000 adults will be there. I asked him why there was such a small number of adults to which he told me that most people as they become adults they forfeit any type of relationship they may have had with God and they either give up on him or engross themselves in religion. Either way, this behavior does not warrant access to the New Jerusalem. I ascertained that many people would have their mansions in the walls of the Holy City and the inside of the place has been described as magical. There are only a handful of adults there right now and the other 3000 will be added at the resurrection. I asked God if he would be willing to add more people, he said he would, and that he would keep the doors open for me to bring more people in. I have two people who are coming on board and God has been blessing one of them immensely, and he lives in one of the poorest countries on earth.

I asked God to describe some of the aspects of the New Jerusalem, and here is what he told me. The city will glisten with his glory, but very few adults will be able to see his glory because of the thick walls - 200 feet thick made of pure gold. The New Jerusalem is a magical place, caves for exploring, mountains to ski, yes, there will be snow on the mountains, all kinds of flowers, fruit trees, gardens, vegetables will be growing all over the place, there will never be a food shortage, ever. There will be rivers and lakes, but there will be no more oceans on the planet, just large bodies of water teeming with life. There will be all kinds of extinct animals that man annihilated and even some dinosaurs will be wandering around, it will be like Jurassic Park only all of the animals will eat grass or other vegetation.

There will be no eating the flesh of animals because everyone will be vegetarians, the animals too, and also the creatures of the big lakes and rivers. We will get around by horses and/or horses and buggies, there will be a way to travel vast distances in a moment of time. Our eyesight will be phenomenal, we will be able to see things clearly at great distances; there will be no eyeglasses or blindness in the Kingdom. It will be much greater than the Garden of Eden ever was.

People will NOT be spending time playing harps in the clouds, no, some will be teaching and taking care of the children. Others will be governing cities within the New Jerusalem. Still, others will learn from the Father about many things because he knows it all. It will be a thriving, bustling, yet peaceful environment. EVERYONE will have an abundance, there will be no money or currency because God will provide everything for free. There will be sports competitions, musicals, concerts, plays, there be many things to do for everybody, no one will be idle. and the Sabbath will be a continual thing. We will have rest for eternity, ***Yom Shekulo Shabbat*** where every day is a beautiful Sabbath rest for us.

When every day is a Sabbath

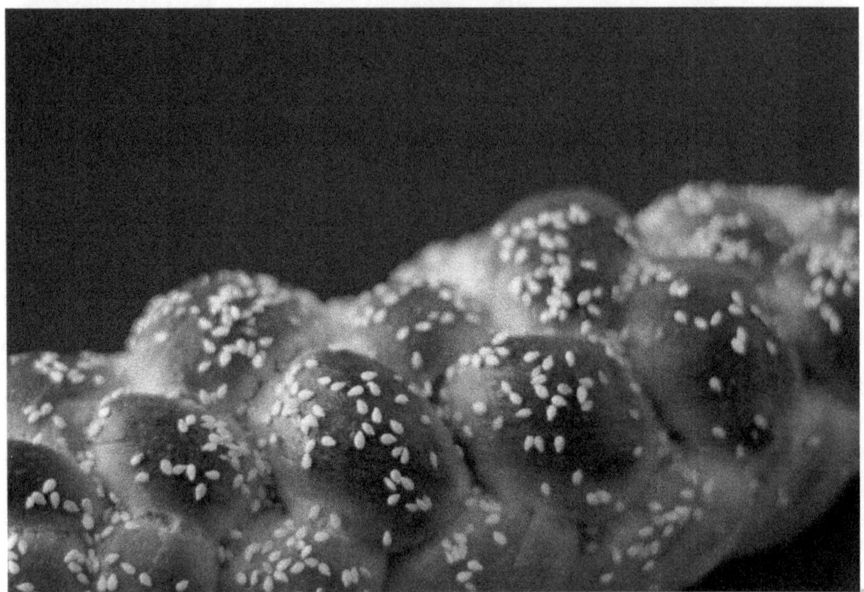

We will eat sweet bread (Challah) and every other delicious food.

The most beautiful aspect of heaven will be our growing relationships with the Father and others. We will have eternity to get to know those who are on the inside. There will be intimate personal fellowship throughout the Kingdom. There will be no need for sex as we will be like the angels, no giving and taking in marriage. Our Father will be the only one some of us are married to. No one will lack anything. There will be no 9-5 grind or having to meet deadlines, nothing like that.

Did you know that you can have some of those aspects here on earth? God told me one day when I was fretting over a deadline and other worries to stop it and realize that I am on His time now. There is no hurrying, no scurrying in the New Jerusalem and peace will flood the city, even cats will be friends with mice. No killing of any kind of creature.

We will be happy all the time. Never sad, never depressed. Once we see God in his glory we will never be the same again. His glory will be so beautiful that there will be times when we just stop and stare at it for hours and hours, speechless because his glory is so beautiful. Words cannot express the beauty of God's glory. There are no words to describe it. The emotions that will come over those of us on the inside when we see his glory will overflow our hearts. We will have a peace that will infinitely surpass anything that we thought was awesome on earth. Consider,

But, as it is written,

"What no eye has seen, nor ear heard,
nor the heart of man imagined,
what God has prepared for those who love him."

To be very honest with you, my feeble attempt to describe the Kingdom of God in the New Jerusalem is infinitely smaller than comparing a pinhead to the known universe. I know nothing about what the New Jerusalem is going to be like. I asked a Catholic Priest who was a friend of mine if there would be ice cream in heaven. I liked his response, he said, if God thinks you need it, it will be there. I love ice cream and I really hope it's there. I wonder if we are going to be lean muscle machines or a bunch of rollie pollies. All I know for sure is that it is going to be tons of fun.

Do the work to ensure you find yourself inside the New Jerusalem.

Next, we are going to look at the final destination for those who say they loved God but did not walk in his ways.

Chapter Four

So, we're looking again at Revelation Chapter 22:15,

For without are dogs, and sorcerers, and whoremongers, and murderers, and idolaters, and whosoever loveth and maketh a lie. Revelation 22:15 KJV

Most people who never followed God with their whole heart, mind, body, and spirit will most likely wind up outside the New Jerusalem. This scripture applies to most Christians, Jews, Muslims, Hindus, Buddhists, New Agers, and basically anyone else who did not pursue a relationship with God. On the first day on the renewed earth and while standing in front of the New Jerusalem, God, or an angel will instruct the billions of people who ever lived on the planet that their new home will be outside the New Jerusalem.

What will he tell these people?

1. They will not be allowed inside the New Jerusalem.
2. There will be some food available, but they will have to farm the land.
3. They will have to build dwellings for themselves.

Outside are the dogs - false teachers and immoral practitioners. The world's religions are full of false teachers and immoral practitioners. Adults who have sex with children, intercourse with animals, male adults who have anal intercourse with other males, those who commit adultery, and any other form of perversion. A false teacher is someone who knowingly promulgates a false doctrine, belief, or ideology. Take, for example, the prosperity gospel where the leader tells the people to give their money to God (actually it's the leader who benefits from this, not God) and he (God) will bless them with an abundance. Some of these leaders make great sums of money from their congregants to the point where the leader becomes extremely wealthy. Some of these people will be labeled as 'the least of these', a people who are on the lowest rung of humans on the renewed earth.

Sorcerers - definition: a person who claims or is believed to have magic powers; a wizard. Sorcerers and those who practice witchcraft will have a very low standing on the renewed earth. There will be no way to practice any form of magic, (I'm not talking about sleight of hand) witchcraft, or sorcery because the sources of magic, black magic, sorcery, and witchcraft will all be in the Lake of Fire. There will be no channeling or consulting the dead because the dead will either be alive in the New Jerusalem, outside the New Jerusalem, or burning in the Lake of Fire.

Whoremongers - definition: a person who has dealings with prostitutes, especially a sexually promiscuous man. The people who frequent whore houses and other forms of prostitution.

Murderers: the unlawful premeditated killing of one human being by another. There will be people labeled as murderers; people who killed other people by malice, torture, abortion, and all other types of murder. These people will have that label stick to them and everyone outside the New Jerusalem will know the company they keep.

Idolaters - Idolatry is the worship of an idol or cult image, being a physical image, such as a statue, or a person in place of God. In Abrahamic religions, namely Judaism, Christianity, and Islam, idolatry connotes the worship of something or someone other than God as if it were God. As you can see, the company on the outside of the New Jerusalem will be very different than those on the inside.

Liars - And whosoever loveth and maketh a lie. The last and final group of people to be placed outside the New Jerusalem will be those people who were in darkness who believed lies and told others the same, or other lies. This group will comprise the majority of Christians, Muslims, and Jews, and other 'spiritual' groups. These are the people who exchanged a true, loving, honest, and genuine relationship with God the Father for religion. They chose to sing about God, pray about God, give money to their leader who they thought was giving to God, who doesn't need a penny from anyone. They went to Bible studies about God, but they never took the time to spend time with Him. They chose religion over relationship. God HATES religion because all it ever did was create division, wars, prejudice, control, perversion, lust, hatred, and many other evil aspects of the darkened satanic and demonic nature of mankind.

There will be terrible regrets by billions of people who thought they were paying God homage by going to a church, mosque, synagogue, or temple. There are no second chances. The regret these people will have will be unbearable but take heart, God will wipe away every tear of regret and the outsiders will get used to living outside in this new environment.

As I understand there will be law and order too. No person on the outside, or inside, for that matter will be allowed to take advantage of others outside the city. Angels will keep the planet secure and will rule with an iron scepter over the inhabitants outside the city. I asked God about the tree of life, which is found inside the New Jerusalem, will there be a tree of life on the outside of the New Jerusalem? He told me that there will be no tree of life on the outside of the New Jerusalem.

It all boils down to the Father's Commandments consider,

For verily I say unto you, Till heaven and earth pass, one jot or one tittle shall in no wise pass from the law, till all be fulfilled. Whosoever therefore shall break one of these least commandments, and shall teach men so, he shall be called the least in the kingdom of heaven: but whosoever shall do and teach them, the same shall be called great in the kingdom of heaven.

So, the Commandments/Law/Instructions/Rules/Torah will not pass away until everything is fulfilled. Let me be very honest with you. The rules of the game of life still apply to us here right now. They will not disappear until we are on the renewed earth. Not everything has been fulfilled yet, so we are still waiting for the return of the Father for his children.

If you are wondering what you must do to inherit a place on the inside of the New Jerusalem I can share with you what the Father has shared with me in my course entitled, These Four Things found here: https://paulcmoore.ca/courses/these-four-things

This course will tell you the four simple things you must do each day to have a successful relationship with your Father in Heaven. I wish you well on your journey and know that everything is going to be okay with you. Get to know your Father in Heaven by doing these four things.

About the Author

Paul Moore is an aspiring author, minister, and prophet. He spent twenty-seven years in organized religion and has been out of the box of religion for seven years. During most of those years he gave huge sums of money to the leaders of congregations he attended. Having been disillusioned with the whole system of religion in 2013, Paul decided to walk away from religion altogether. It has been liberating for him as he now seeks God without having to go through a middleman. Instead, he has a direct line to the Father whereby he can communicate with him in what the Bible calls the still small voice of God. This is a gift he treasures and in time desires to see the whole world awakened to who our Father in Heaven really is.

You can visit his personal website at: https://paulcmoore.ca

Paul has an umbrella organization called Happy Life Family Fellowship International, which is an alternative to church attendance, with branches in Uganda and Canada. You can view the Happy Life Family Fellowship International website at, https://hlffi.org

Look for more books by Paul C Moore at his Amazon author page,

https://amazon.com/author/paulcmoore

Paul also has an orphanage that he supports in Uganda and you can access it here, https://ucoff.org

www.ingramcontent.com/pod-product-compliance
Lightning Source LLC
LaVergne TN
LVHW010511160826
845677LV00012B/2790